C000056456

LEAN & ᴸᴱᴬᴺ

SIX SIGMA

FOR PROJECT

MANAGEMENT

Peter Oliver

LEAN & LEAN SIX SIGMA

Copyright © 2018 by Concise Reads™

TABLE OF CONTENTS

INTRODUCTION

"To produce only what is needed, when it is needed and in the amount needed" -- Taiichi Ohno

In the previous Concise Reads, we discovered the framework for Agile software development. We learned that the purpose of rapid prototyping was to reduce inefficiency and build a customer valued product through efficiency gains from experienced development. Agile was the necessary framework to build a product, but in order to build a company that scales we need to learn about the concepts of streamlining a business process taught in the frameworks of Lean and Six Sigma.

To simplify our understanding of how these frameworks work together we have created the following simple schema of the product value chain:

AGILE → LEAN → LEAN SIX SIGMA

When first creating a new product, a product manager would start with AGILE. There is a concept known as Lean Startup popularized by Eric Ries that promotes building a minimum viable product, shipping it to customers, getting their feedback and then iterating multiple times. It borrows the same concept of rapid prototyping as Agile but is much less structured. Unlike Agile, Lean Startup focuses on testing each iteration with end customers until the right product-market fit is eventually found. Lean Startup's 'Build, Measure, Learn' loop is often placed between initial design thinking of what the product is going to be and Agile which speeds up the development cycle for a larger project build.

When the product is market ready, the focus shifts on reducing costs and maximizing operational efficiency through the use of LEAN principles. For an introduction to operations management as used in manufacturing processes see the Concise Reads 'Operations Management'.

For a commercial ready product whose processes have been fine-tuned using LEAN, we then turn to SIX SIGMA to minimize variation. It is not typical of early stage companies to employ SIX SIGMA as there are marginally greater gains from employing AGILE or LEAN. However, for larger enterprises, SIX SIGMA is so valued that corporate training is paid for the first introduction to six sigma (YELLOW BELT) all the way to the masters of the framework (MASTER BLACK BELT). It's definitely a resume filler.

Fortunately, in this Concise Reads book, we will simplify Lean and Six Sigma so that you can walk away with a deeper de-mystified understanding and appreciation of the tools and all in an hour or less. We won't cover the statistical tools of Six Sigma as those require weeks and months of formal teaching, but you will walk away with a better sense if this is something you want to pursue further with more advanced training.

LEAN

Lean is a framework to reduce waste and improve operations efficiency. It is a never-ending process of waste removal, therefore it promotes a continuous chain of improvements.

It is a management philosophy borrowed from the Toyota Production System (TPS). A person unfamiliar with the advantages of Lean may ask why is there a need to learn a framework? If something is broken, we can just fix it then and there. To that I remind the reader that Socrates went around asking the smartest people a series of questions until the point where they did not have the answer to his questions. He then proclaimed that he is probably the smartest person alive because at least he knows that he knows nothing.

The Lean framework teaches us what to look for, and how to look for it. I'd like you to embrace Lean as a way to discover waste and inefficiency—more efficiently.

THE TOYOTA 3M MODEL

Waste is the enemy of Lean. The enemy has three heads:

1) Muda ('futility'),
2) Mura ('unevenness'), and
3) Muri ('overburden').

Muda is the largest and most obvious head of this enemy, but cutting that head only temporarily slows down the enemy as a new head grows out of the smaller Mura and Muri heads. If you decide to cut off either the Mura or Muri heads, then all you did was stop the growth of Muda and possibly put it into a slow regression. If you really want to defeat the enemy, you have to find all three heads. I use the analogy of the three-headed enemy because as you'll see, it's not easy to forget.

Let's look at the three types of waste:

1. **Muda:** translates to 'futility'. Muda is the most obvious type of <u>waste</u> that is not value-added, or in other words, it does not increase the probability that your customer will pay for or pay a higher price for your product. The most common types of Muda are defective production and excess or idle inventory. There are 8 Muda's which we will cover in this guide: <u>D</u>efects, <u>O</u>verproduction, <u>W</u>aiting, <u>N</u>on-utilized talent, <u>T</u>ransportation, <u>I</u>nventory, <u>M</u>otion, <u>E</u>xtra Processing (Acronym: "DOWNTIME")

2. **Mura:** translates to 'unevenness' which is seen when there is fluctuation in process times for the same product, uneven customer demand, or uneven productivity

of different shift workers (also known as cycle time per worker). This unevenness creates <u>uncertainty</u>, which ultimately affects the efficacy of the supply chain (both before and after the step with Mura). This is similar to Six Sigma's focus on reducing variation, but while Six Sigma reduces variation to improve quality, Lean reduces Mura to <u>prevent waste (Muda)</u> from occurring.

3. **Muri:** literally translates to 'overburden'. Overutilization of machines or employees leads to waste events in the form of machine breakdowns or employee absenteeism for stress, injury, or even job dissatisfaction. To combat Muri, preventative maintenance and employee safety measures are of the utmost importance. Additionally, if companies can

afford it, shifting repetitive manual work to automated machines decreases Muri of employees.

Mura and Muri are not wastes but <u>causes</u> of waste (Muda) and must be eliminated to prevent Muda.

FIVE PRINCIPLES OF LEAN

The term Lean was coined by John Krafcik in his 1988 article, "Triumph of the Lean Production System". Krafcik worked as an engineer with Toyota which over the 20th century has improved the production process by focusing on Muda, Mura, and Muri.

There are five principles in Lean, and those are: Value, Value Stream, Flow, Pull, and Perfection.

VALUE: The product and process depend on the value created for the end consumer. The first step is therefore to identify important parameters of value for the customer as well as align those values with the corporate strategy. If corporate strategy is to produce high quality products, and the customer expects high quality products, then focusing business unit tactical strategy and lower level operations on reducing the defect rate is not only value-added, but of <u>higher value</u> relative to others.

In Agile we built a customer-centric product focusing on the must haves versus the should and could haves. This is the same process. If we know exactly what brings value to the customer, then we can make sure to remove everything else that does not. Lean does not focus on prioritization of value-added products as much as Agile, but I recommend ranking the value added features qualitatively or quantitatively if you have limited resources.

VALUE STREAM: The value stream is the entire process from manufacturing to distribution to use and disposal of the product by the end consumer. This end-to-end process maps out the steps from request to delivery. To eliminate waste, we must break down the product and processes into value-added and non-value-added parts. In the Lean world, drawing out all the steps is called **Value Stream Mapping (VSM)**. It's not difficult. The only thing to keep in mind is to draw out everything including the flow of product as well as the flow of information (i.e. What happens once a customer places an order? How is that order recorded?).

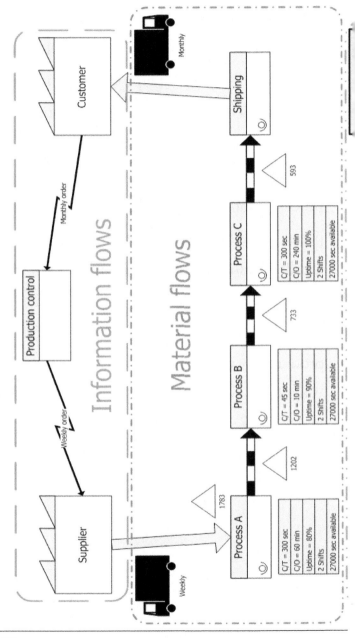

What is needed to identify waste is **data**. Data is a key component of the modern Lean tool belt. There are over 100 different Lean tools to measure and display different types of data. As you delve into more advanced coursework in Lean and also begin with your first VSM, you will find new metrics that are important for your industry or process. At minimum, you should document these data points in a data box as shown in the previous figure. Some common data points for each step or process are:

- Capacity: total capacity per unit of time.

- Up-time: on-demand machine utilization cycle time; typically, less than 100% because there is some waste such as waste of motion.

- Cycle time (CT): how long each step takes.

☐ Wait time between steps.

☐ Total lead time from start to finish.

☐ WIP inventory: In the figure it is depicted as a triangle between steps with number of units in inventory.

☐ Number of operators.

☐ Number of shifts.

☐ Scrap rate.

☐ Batch size.

An important metric and one of my favorites (as discussed in the Operations Management Concise Reads) is **Takt time**. It sets the rhythm or pace of production based on customer demand. It is the maximum time between starting production of one product and when the next product needs to start to meet demand. For example, if I work 40 hours a week and my customer demand is 80 units per week, then 40/80=0.5 hours. That means that to meet demand, my lead time cannot exceed 0.5 hours in a pure pull production system where I produce units only when demanded by customers. I always add Takt time to any VSM or process mapping (same as VSM but focuses on identifying at a high level whether each process step is value added instead of focusing on the measurement of waste using data).

The more data the better, but instead of trying to fit other people's metrics, it is better to improve upon the metrics you chose with each iteration (Kaizen; continuous improvement).

Armed with data, now you are ready to identify waste. Let's tackle that next.

While originally consisting of 7 wastes in the Toyota Production System (TPS), James Womack and Daniel Jones added the 8th waste of talent (or human capital) in their 2003 publication 'Lean Thinking: Banish Waste and Create Wealth in Your Corporation'. Womack and Jones are also the authors along with Daniel Roos of the worldwide popular 1990 book 'The Machine That Changed The World' which first coined Lean Production and which became a must-read for any MBA student since then.

The 8 wastes (Muda) are recalled with the acronym **DOWNTIME** as follows:

Defects: defects are pure cost. The customer is not going to pay for them, and defective production is non-value added.

Over processing: over processing that does not add value will not be paid for by the customer. Additionally, over processing can lead to other wastes such as wasteful motion. Imagine a sales order that has to be verified by several people before it actually makes it to the factory. Maybe the second verification helps ensure the right product is made and reduces error but if the additional verifications do not add value, then they are waste in the form of overprocessing.

Waiting: waiting is a common non-value-added activity and one that slows down flow. Ideally, the simplest solution is a redesign of processes so that flow is demand driven with each step 'pulling' the intermediate product as soon as they are ready. Too much waiting, and you are faced with inventory buildup which is another form waste. In queuing theory, application of this pull principle is seen in single file lines for multiple counters which reduces Lead time compared to different queues for different counters. That is why we see a long single line at airport security checkpoints and even at the local fast food retailer.

Non-used employee talent: This is simple enough to understand. I like to use the analogy of two guys and a truck moving company where the 5'3" thin employee is the one moving the furniture and the 6'5" heavily muscled employee is the one driving the truck! That is a waste of muscle talent. Taking inventory of employee skills and productivity is important to eliminate the waste of idle talent.

Transportation: Delivery is the only transportation that a customer will pay for. All else is waste and must be minimized. Sam Walton of Walmart was ingenious in his choice of strategic location for his warehouses. He further reduced waste by filling every truck to maximum capacity and re-loading the truck soon after unloading on the same dock to reduce wasted motion (another form of waste).

Inventory: the science behind inventory management and distribution is so advanced that there are third party vendors offering logistics services to larger corporations. Some tried and true methods include the pull production system we've previously mentioned, small lot production, and Just-In-Time (JIT) inventory. Of course, to reduce the waste of inventory, you need good data across your supply chain. Walmart stores built a communication system that allowed warehouses earlier in the supply chain to be notified when inventory was low at a specific store. They also have analytics that help them forecast how long they have remaining before the inventory at a specific store would be completely sold out thereby dictating when and how much to produce, purchase, or deliver.

Motion: waste from excess motion is very common. Often times, we don't even realize it. Data on time spent moving from one station to another will help make the waste discoverable. The best illustration of waste from excess motion is that made of a typical farmer by Henry Ford in his book 'My Life And Work':

"I believe that the average farmer puts to a really useful purpose only about 5% of the energy that he spends. …Not only is everything done by hand, but seldom is a thought given to logical arrangement. A farmer doing his chores will walk up and down a rickety ladder a dozen times. He will carry water for years instead of putting in a few lengths of pipe."

Excessive Production (also known as overproduction): This is an interesting form of waste. It clearly leads to inventory pile up, some of which may never get sold if customer demand changes and the company is forced to produce version 2.0 of the product. Yet, in most episodes of Shark Tank, we find the new entrepreneurs asking for a capital raise to manufacture in bulk and bring costs down. This is push production. The Sharks hate that reasoning. The best way to scale a business is to set the price at what the consumer wants then begin production to meet demand. As demand increases, production volume increases, and costs decreases. This means a short period of time where profits are small or none, but ensures there is no waste. This combines small lot production and pull production tools. What the Sharks do love is when an entrepreneur comes in with letters of interest (LOIs) or confirmed purchase orders which need to be filled. There is a big difference here.

FLOW: Flow is directly related to the value stream. The only reason it's set apart is to focus your efforts on mapping the value stream in the second step, and then to focus on flow parameters between each step ensuring that there is no interruption to flow. With no interruption to flow, there is no wait time, there is no inventory, and no excess production. That's 3 of the 8 Mudas. The other 5 need a closer inspection of the process that flow parameters don't directly identify. The flow parameters to measure include **cycle time** per step, **wait time**, **lead time**, **capacity**, **output**, and **demand**. If we remember from the 'Operations Management' Concise Reads, lead time is the total time from order to a finished product (or delivery if that is a final stage).

Henry Ford reduced lead time to build a car from 12 hours to 2.5 hours with introduction of the assembly line and process improvements to reduce wasted motion.

PULL: Pull production is a foundational principle of Lean. The problem with pull production is that it requires a lot of flexibility to implement an order-then-build approach as well as clear visibility throughout the value stream. The good news is that we live in a time where technology has made communication along the value stream as simple as an order popping up on a screen from the consumer down to the first step in the supply chain. To make a pull production system successful, cycle times need to be short and lead time needs to be sufficiently short to satisfy the consumer. With a pull production system, the work-in-process (WIP) inventory, or inventory pile up in any of the steps, should be significantly reduced.

PERFECTION: The 5th and final principle is perfection, or more accurately the 'pursuit' of perfection. It's likely described this way to appeal to a western audience, but the roots of this principle are based in the Japanese Kaizen or continuous improvement. Kaizen is a mindset that requires us to adapt quickly. When Mike Tyson was asked whether he had a fight plan for his upcoming fight with Evander Holyfield, he famously said "everyone has a plan until they get punched in the mouth". Kaizen means you are nimble enough to adapt your plans if your product gets punched in the mouth.

Kaizen practitioners use the PDCA cycle (also known as Deming or Shewhart or control cycle). It stands for Plan, Do, Check, Adjust (or Act). Originally described by William Edwards Deming, it has its roots in the scientific method of hypothesis-experiment-evaluation. Deming later modified PDCA to PDSA changing the 'Check' to 'Study' because he felt people where not analyzing the data. This brings me back to data and something I want etched in your memory.

When you identify waste, and you use PDSA to problem solve a solution, you must measure different data metrics to feed the next iteration of PDSA. The process is simple.

Identify a waste, pick a standard or benchmark that you want to improve (such as cycle time or WIP inventory) and then **plan** a small improvement, **do** the small improvement, **study** the new data as well as the benchmark metric. If the new plan improved the benchmark metric, then use the new benchmark or standard as the next baseline for the next PDSA cycle and if it didn't then **adjust** the plan and so on. Looks very familiar to Scrum sprints from the prior Concise Reads! That's because it is.

There are many ways to problem solve a new plan other than PDSA. Some common ones are described in the earlier guide in the series 'Problem Solving'. The takeaway is that your first attempt at Lean will not be the last one, and that's why Lean is a life-long skill for managers.

THE PRINCIPLES SHORTCUT

When embarking on a Lean Transformation, we would set up a team that would go through the 5 principles of Lean previously stated. Each PDSA cycle can take hours or weeks depending on the process. However, what if you're a solo entrepreneur running a coffee shop? What is a quick method to apply lean methodology? Well you're in luck, because Womack and Jones described three important considerations--**Purpose, Process, People,** to shortcut the identification of waste.

Marcus Lemonis of the show 'The Profit' also uses the same shortcut to evaluate how much waste a small business has before deciding if he can reduce (and profit from it)--except he calls it **Product** instead of **Purpose**.

Purpose/Product is the value the company is delivering to the customer. Is the customer getting the value they are paying for?

Process: Is there a clear flow for each step in the value stream? Are all the steps adding value?

People: Are the people empowered (and interested) to make continuous improvement adjustments? Are their talents maximized? What do they think would improve the flow?

The reason Marcus focuses on these three considerations is because he knows as did Benjamin Franklin and Henry Ford before him that reducing waste (and therefore costs) is a surer path to profit than focusing on revenue first.

LEAN TOOLKIT:

Now that we understand the three enemies of Lean—Muda, Mura, and Muri—and also understand the 5 principles of Lean Transformation (value, value stream, flow, pull, perfection), we can describe some of the tools used to reduce waste.

1. Defects:

    a. **Poka Yoke (mistake proofing):** is the Japanese method of pre-emptively eliminating the possibility of building defective products. There are two types of Poka Yoke. **Warning systems** which alert the employee when there is an outlier or deviation from a normal range or standard, and **control systems** which are fail safes that automatically arrest a machine when there is a deviation from the normal range. Computer systems are built using Poka Yoke, where a warning system could alert the user of a potential malicious site and control systems would turn off the computer when it overheats to prevent further damage. There is a similar concept in Six Sigma called <u>control charts</u> which we will cover in this guide.

b. **Standard work** requires the delineation of what is considered normal as part of the task's Standard Operating Procedure or **SOP**. In healthcare, SOPs come in the form of checklists so that regardless of the operator, the result should be the same (thereby also minimizing Mura or variability). There is a checklist for everything in healthcare from the supplies used in the operating room to the medications used in recovery. This is because defects in healthcare are unacceptable. As an aside, despite the best intentions, defects do occur, and they are called 'never events'. Never events include performing surgery on the wrong patient or the wrong side. Whether SOPs or checklists are used, clearly defining the steps for each process minimizes potential for defects.

2. Over Processing: There is such as a thing as unnecessary work.

a. **Process Mapping:** When building the value stream map, be sure to focus on the processes involved with each step and then define it as value-added or non-value-added. Over processing is not measured by cycle time or WIP inventory buildup because you are looking to justify the entire process step based on the end customer needs. The simplest example is finding that an employee spends 20% putting together the content for a business unit meeting and 80% of their time on formatting a PowerPoint deck to make it look pleasing. The question then becomes, does the end consumer of this document care about the design and look of the deck? If not, then it is a non-value-added process—an example of over processing that creates waste.

3. Waiting:

   a. **Time Studies:** To measure waiting we start with measuring **cycle time (CT)** which is how long a step or process takes. We then measure **lead time (LT)** which is how long it takes from start to a finished product. CT/LT is our **operational efficiency**. 1- CT/LT is the percentage of waste from waiting. Waiting is the time a product waits to be pulled to the next step.

b. **Takt Time:** My favorite metric. Because Takt time tells us how much we <u>should</u> produce given customer demand at a point in time, we automatically know that if production is faster than Takt time then we will have products in inventory which is a waste, and if production is slower than Takt time then the customer ends up waiting which is bad for business.

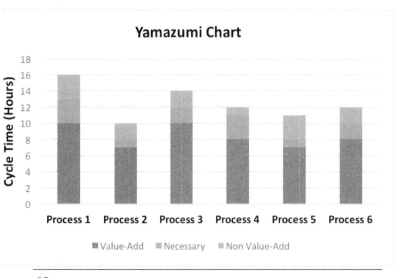

Yamazumi Chart

c. **Yamazumi Chart:** The Yamazumi chart is a stacked chart with cycle time (CT) in the y-axis and the different steps or processes in the x-axis. Each process has a bar that displays value-added work, necessary work (but no direct value added), and non-value-added work. This visual helps the manager decide on optimal line balancing. For example, if the CT of step 3 is longer than the CT of step 2 then there will waiting between the two steps. To eliminate the waste of waiting, which is not depicted in the bar chart but assumed if the bars are uneven, then steps can be re-arranged or step 3's non-value added work can be reduced to balance it, or step 3 can be duplicated so now you have two step 3s if it is twice as slow as step 2.

You get the idea. Is it helpful when you only have two steps? Not really, but when you have multiple steps to produce a product, a visual representation like the Yamazumi chart is helpful to decide where to reduce waste first and to attempt line balancing.

4. Non-Used Talent: Better termed as misused talent but we needed an 'N' to fit the DOWNTIME acronym.

a. **Training:** Assuming you made the right decisions and hired the right people for the job, then the next step to make sure they maximize their potential is through training. Toyota and GE (two great examples of companies that employ Lean) invest heavily in training. The basic training that all workers or at least line managers should have includes Kaizen mindset, Kanban board (to keep a pulse on the flow of product or development), value stream mapping, adhering to a standard work document, and the 5S Lean tool to avoid interruptions and make it easier to detect the causes of waste. We discussed the aforementioned tools except for **5S** which is a methodology made up of 5 Japanese words to bring order to a messy workplace environment. Let's explore each one next.

b. **Seiri (sort):** remove any items that are not used; store items that are infrequently used. Adopt minimalism.

c. **Seiton (straighten):** organize items to optimize efficiency. If a worker uses 5 tools for one part of the product and 2 tools for the other, then 5 tools should be grouped in one section of the workplace and the other tools grouped for the other section. Similarly, if the worker stores an object they use often in a top shelf where they have to use a ladder, then that object should be moved closer. Heavy objects should be made easier to move with a wheelbase.

When Seiton is employed methodically, you will be amazed at the reduction of wasted motion.

d. **Seiso (shine):** Clean the workspace before leaving and always keep it clean so as to easily identify problems or causes of waste. All missing items should be collected and organized before leaving. Clean workspaces also increase productivity.

e. **Seiketsu (standardize):** standardize as much as you can in the workspace (similar to the Lean standard work tool). Large companies that have multiple different types of engineers offer color coded jackets or hard hats to differentiate who's who. Doctors wear long white coats, medical students wear short white coats. Similarly, items meant for one department versus another can be tagged with color coding or with symbols.

f. **Shitsuke (sustain):** This is the hardest of the 5S methodology. Once implemented, make sure to sustain the changes through continuous training and periodic evaluation. Eventually, these behaviors become formed habits and part of the company culture.

5. Transport: While motion focuses on individual motion, transport includes transport of people, product, or information.

   a. **Spaghetti Diagram:** very simple tool. If you are looking to reduce waste of transportation within a facility for example, then you would draw a rough map of the facility with pointed arrows drawing the movement of product, people, or information. If a receiving node has a single arrow to it, then it makes sense to reduce transportation by moving that closer to the location of the sending node (or vice versa). If multiple lines cross, then rearrange the receiving nodes, chart new non-intersecting paths, or change the time of day of different transported items. That's it!

I would like to take this opportunity to tell you about Taiichi Ohno's **Chalk Circle**. Taiichi Ohno was a VP at Toyota who is credited as one of the founders of the Toyota Production System (TPS). He was a difficult guy to get along with, rumored to have a harsh treatment of his managers. One day, a manager came to him with a problem in one of the processes or steps on the factory floor. Ohno drew a circle with chalk in the center of that process and told the manager to stay there and observe until he found the solution. A few hours later, he came back and the manager couldn't solve the problem he initially brought up, so Ohno told him to stay in that circle until he figured it out. He did this with many different managers during his tenure, and it is rumored to have worked.

Observation is the first step in many problem solving tools. Operations consultants often spend the first few days of their engagement with a client just observing every process from A to Z and documenting each step and each movement of people and items.

Documentaries about native tribes of any continent are often filmed observations with a voice-over in post-production to explain what is happening. Policer officers and mall caps are literally <u>trained</u> observers. Observation is tried and true but now we have technology with cameras on the shop floor, GPS trackers on trucks, and serialization of products to track them through the supply chain. Still, keep a chalk handy just in case, but put yourself in the circle instead as the manager in charge.

b. **Production lines and work-cells:** production lines are linear, and work-cells are in a U-shape with input and output appearing on the same end of the U. These are two factory layouts to reduce transportation waste.

6. Inventory:

   a. **Reduce uncertainty:** inventory can build up if there is demand uncertainty which affects the accuracy of forecasting production needs. Try to get letters of interest or better yet purchase orders in advance so you could produce exactly what is needed when it is needed.

b. **Reduce batch size and lead time:**
Larger batches increase lead time which makes forecasting more difficult because you have to forecast farther in the future than with a smaller batch size. Additionally, larger batch sizes also mean larger WIP inventory. Similarly, achieving a shorter lead time by removing waste results in better matching of production and customer demand.

7. Motion: Tools to help reduce motion include the 5S, standard work, and spaghetti diagrams. The key here is to begin with observation, since that is the only tool you have to measure motion directly. A fun exercise used by Lean teachers is to ask their students to make buttered toast or a peanut butter sandwich and record themselves in the kitchen. Then employ Lean tools like 5S to reduce motion. It only takes a few minutes, so you might as well try it now. You'll see that you have to find the tools you need (knife, toaster, butter, toaster), that they're located in different places, and that you always have to look for them. I use the principle of Seiketsu (standardize) for my morning coffee. I have the coffee, cream, sugar, spoon, mug, and kettle all in the same location and near the sink. After I'm done, I wash the mug and put it in the same place thereby continuing to

minimize motion for the next round of caffeine fuel.

8. Excess Production:

   a. **Pull Production:** we're familiar with pull production so I won't belabor it. Using a Kanban board or system helps provide the signals that a new product is ready to be pulled. Additionally, if you have multiple workers doing the same type of job, it is great to have them pull from the same location similar to a single line with multiple registers in queuing theory.

b. **SMED:** Single Minute Exchange of Die. This relates to reducing the changeover (retooling) of a machine or workspace to produce a different product or to reduce the maintenance time. Toyota developed it to reduce the changeover of their machines on the factory floor. At first, this might not seem to relate to excess production, but it does—indirectly. Changeover causes lost productivity which forces companies to produce larger batches. By reducing changeover, the company is now able to produce smaller batches which as we learned improves forecasting thereby reducing inventory buildup and allows for responsiveness to customer demand if a different product needs to be produced. To implement SMED, you need to identify which parts of the changeover need to be done when all work has stopped on a machine or workspace (termed as **'internal'**) and which can be done separately or **'external'**. Then remove parts of the changeover that are waste. Then streamline and optimize the process by getting the external work completed separately such as having the needed tools ready, or using parallel work. SMED was developed by Shigeo Shingo, a Japanese industrial engineer and found average reduction in changeover times of 94%! Some literature reference him as a mentor to Taiichi Ohno who was one of the founders of the TPS.

LEAN SIX SIGMA

Six Sigma was developed in 1986 by Bill Smith at Motorola as a tool for <u>quality control</u>. Six Sigma became popular once Jack Welch introduced it to GE in 1996 with a reported $10 billion in savings within the first 5 years. Six Sigma is a limit (arbitrarily set) on the tolerance limit for manufactured goods. Assuming measures of quality fall on a normal distribution, then outliers are identified as those that are Six Sigma or six standard deviations from the mean. A modified Six Sigma took into account that the mean can shift by 1.5 standard deviations on either side depending on the sample used. Six Sigma is about 3.4 defects per million events which is pretty negligible depending on the industry. The problem with Six Sigma is that it's a theoretical goal to achieve very high quality but not one that considers more immediate cost considerations.

That is why Lean Six Sigma uses Lean methodology to reduce waste and Six Sigma to better reduce variation (Mira) which leads to defects or waste eventually.

<u>Six Sigma today implies *Lean* Six Sigma.</u>

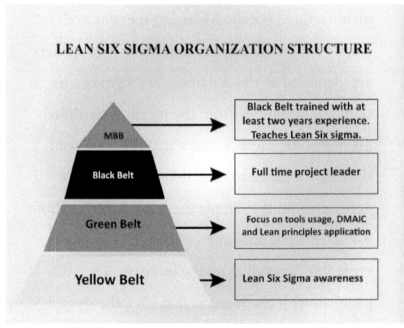

LEAN SIX SIGMA ORGANIZATION STRUCTURE

MBB → Black Belt trained with at least two years experience. Teaches Lean Six sigma.

Black Belt → Full time project leader

Green Belt → Focus on tools usage, DMAIC and Lean principles application

Yellow Belt → Lean Six Sigma awareness

In 1987, Dr. Mikel Harry came up with the black belt certification which popularized the Six Sigma courses. The levels from newbie to champion are as follows: Yellow Belt, Green Belt, Black Belt, Master Black Belt, and finally Champion or Project Sponsor.

SIGMA PERFORMANCE LEVELS

When describing the performance level of a process, Six Sigma students call it Sigma 1-6. This is based on the calculation of the defect ratio for a sample multiplied by a million to get the Defects Per Million Opportunities or DPMO. Opportunities are the total number of occurrences or events. To give you a real-world example—flight crashes occur 1 in 1.2 million flights which is Sigma level > 6. On the other hand, car crashes occur for every 130 people out of every 100,000 population each year. That's a rate of 1300 DPMO or between Sigma level 4 and 5. A table is included here for reference.

Sigma Level	Defects Per Million Opportunities (DPMO)
1	690,000
2	308,537
3	66,807
4	6,210
5	233
6	3.4

TOOLS OF QUALITY

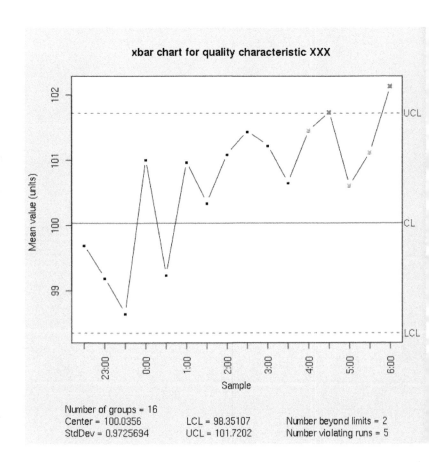

Control Chart: Walter Shewhart developed the control charts in 1924 and is considered the founder of the concept of statistical quality control. To create a control chart, we pick a quality measure such as defects and plot it in a chart as shown in the example. Then we specify the upper and lower control limits to identify what's **normal** variation. Typically, that is set at 3 standard deviations above and below the mean or average control limit (CL). We then expect that **68%** of points will fall within 1 standard deviation, **95%** within 2 standard deviations, and **99.7%** within 3 standard deviations. If a point or number of points are outside this expectation of a normal distribution then we would identify it as abnormal or **special** variation, and that will alert us that something has changed or was introduced that caused this variation. For example, if we have 100 points of observation then we expect only 0.3% or <1 points to be outside of 3 standard deviations and 5% or about 5 points outside of 2 standard deviations. If we find 3 points are above the 3-standard deviation line or the upper control limit, then something is off. Similarly, if 10 points are above the 2-standard deviation line, then again something is off, and we need to investigate the cause. Additionally, if all the points are within 1 standard deviation, there isn't enough normal variation which should prompt us to take a closer look. To do that we can use an Ishikawa diagram or any number of problem solving methods to find the root cause.

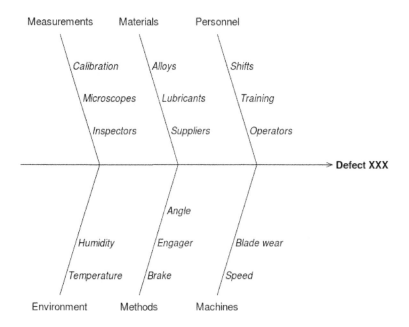

Factors contributing to defect XXX

Ishikawa diagram: Also known as a fishbone or cause-and-effect diagram. Kaoru Ishikawa popularized this root cause analysis method in the 1960s while working for Kawasaki. The defect is depicted as the fish head and each rib off the backbone consists of one of the five major causes for defects in manufacturing with sub-branches for components of the major cause. The 5 major causes also known as **5M** are Machine, Method (process), Material, Man (personnel), and

Measurement. Other major causes often included are Mission (environment), Management, and Maintenance. This differs depending on product and industry. I wouldn't focus on this except to understand that breaking up a problem into its components helps us identify the root cause. If we can break up major causes into minor ones, then even better.

**For additional problem-solving techniques that can be applied to any industry, see the Concise Reads 'Problem Solving'.

DMAIC

Lean Six Sigma uses Lean to expose waste and Six Sigma to reduce variation (and ultimately improve quality). Six Sigma methodologies are based off of William Deming's PDCA or PDSA cycle to identify root causes and continuously improve through repeated iterations of the cycle. The two most common tools are DMAIC to reduce variation in existing processes and DMADV to minimize variation for planned processes. DMAIC spells out:

1. **Define:** similar to Agile and Lean, we need to define the **Voice of the Customer (VOC).** Specifically, we explicitly define what is value added and what is not. We use those to compare to the measurements from our process or the **Voice of the Process (VOP).** Because it's Six Sigma, we also identify the **Critical To Quality (CTQ)** values which we use in the next step.

2. **Measure:** Data informs. Therefore, we calculate metrics for the process. In terms of quality, we focus on defect rate, and process capability (described in the next section).

3. **Analyze:** this is straight forward. We are comparing the measured data and then identifying root causes by employing basic problem solving like asking 'why?' and drawing a fishbone diagram to determine cause and effect.

4. **Improve:** We employ lean principles such as poka yoke, standard work, and 5S to reduce variation.

5. **Control:** Similar to establishing a benchmark to continuously monitor improvement in the PDSA cycle, we build control systems such as the **statistical process control (SPC)** which maps the distribution of variation in what is known as a **control chart** to distinguish 'common' variation which has a predictable pattern and can be considered normal and expected to 'special' variation which has a non-predictable pattern. A common variation is a 'stable' process (i.e predictable) and a process capability study can be used to detect early warning signs if a process will not be capable of meeting customer quality expectations.

There are several statistical calculations learned through each of the Six Sigma certifications. It is beyond the scope of this introductory concise reads, but to give you a sense, let's describe what a process capability metric is.

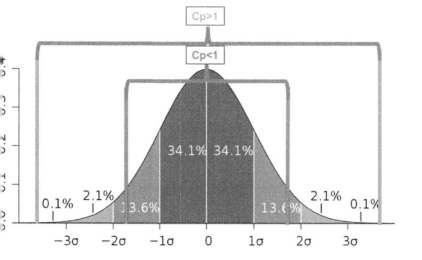

The **process capability** is the application of statistical **specification limits** to be able to tell if a production will meet **quality** expectations. For example, a process capability study can take a control chart with enough data points (means of a quality metric for example such as mean defects), draw a frequency normal distribution as shown and impose how much variation a customer is willing to accept. A process capability ratio is simply dividing the width of the specification limits or customer expectation by the width of 6 standard deviations of the distribution (3 standard deviation on either side of the mean). Anything less than one means the process is not 'capable' of meeting customer expectation. Because the expectation is that the process will vary by 3 standard deviations, then it will not fall within the customer specifications (see CP<1). In the special case where the mean specification limit is not equal to the mean of the distribution, that implies that the distribution is shifted either to the lower limit or higher limit of the specification level. In this case, we calculate the width of one end of the specification limit from the mean divided by the width of 3 standard deviations from the mean and repeat for the other side. We then pick the smaller number of the two ratios. That is known as a **process capability index**.

Specific training is obtained through Six Sigma certifications but the point for control systems is that early detection allows for early correction before the problem becomes worse.

DMADV

Also known as DFSS or Design for Six Sigma.

1. **Define:** Identify Voice of Customer (VOC)

2. **Measure:** Identify metrics that are Critical To Quality (CTQs). This depends on the product being manufactured.

3. **Analyze:** Analyze multiple alternatives that would maximize CTQs.

4. **Design:** Map out the optimal production design.

5. **Verify:** Run a pilot study to verify the simulated analysis results from two steps prior.

DFSS uses statistical software to model processes and simulate variation with different inputs. It significantly reduces the risk of more costly process changes down the line. It is heavily used in the auto-industry to design processes with acceptable variability for production of a new model car. DMADV can be thought of as a statistical version of operations research. It's training is also based on the Six Sigma ranking system with Yellow, Green, and Black belt certifications.

CONCLUSION

This is a rather longer Concise Reads than usual, but I figured I might as well group Lean and Six Sigma together, so you can learn it all in one day. The lessons are intuitive but sometimes you need to read the explanation once more to understand it. Remember the three-headed enemy of Lean: Muda, Mura, and Muri. Know the 8 forms of Muda or waste as well as the 5 Lean principles which are the sequential steps used if you were to start a Lean Transformation project.

The 5 Lean principles again are:
1. Value: Focus on customer needs
2. Value Stream: Identify waste
3. Flow: Meet customer needs by eliminating waste and having continuous flow

4. Pull: Make sure production is dictated by customer demand not production capacity; Employ Kanban

5. Perfection: Employ Kaizen continuous improvement

Six Sigma can be grouped into the last principle of lean, that of Kaizen by using DMAIC to identify and eliminate the cause of abnormal variation (Mura). DFSS is used in pre-production with solutions to reduce variation tested on simulated statistical models.

Hope you enjoyed this quick guide, for any additional topics in management, be sure to send us a request by email.

Additionally, some helpful books for further reading include:

1. The Lean Six Sigma Pocket Toolbook by Michael George
2. The Toyota Way by James Womack
3. The Machine That Changed The World by James Womack

For information on Six Sigma certifications, see https://www.iassc.org/